Music Minus One Vocals

Broadway Hits

for Tenor

2145

Broadway Hits for Tenor

CONTENTS

ISBN 978-1-941566-45-9

Younger Than Springtime

from "South Pacific"

Words and Music by
Richard Rodgers & Oscar Hammerstein

MMO 2145

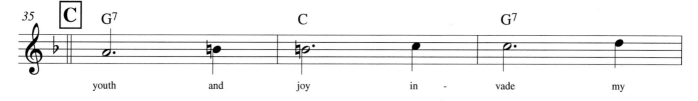

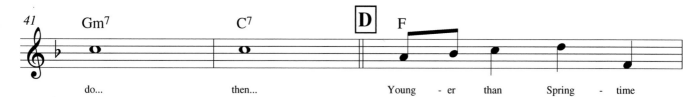

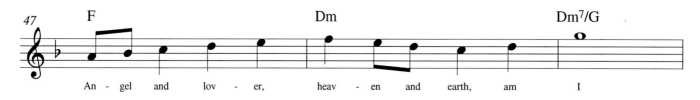

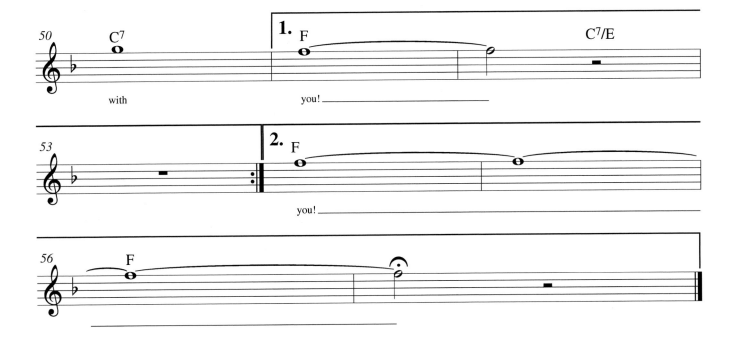

Miracle of Miracles

from "Fiddler On The Roof"

Words and Music by
Jerry Bock and Sheldon Harnick

8

Oh, What A Beautiful Mornin'

from "Oklahoma"

Words and Music by
Richard Rodgers & Oscar Hammerstein

MMO 2145

It Ain't Necessarily So
from "Porgy & Bess"

Words and Music by
George Gershwin, Ira Gershwin,
Dorothy Heyward, Du bose, Heyward

Till Good Luck Comes My Way

from "Show Boat"

Words and Music by
Jerome Kern and Oscar Hammerstein

You've Got To Be Carefully Taught
from "South Pacific"

Words and Music by
Richard Rodgers & Oscar Hammerstein

MMO 2145

The Highest Judge Of All
from "Carousel"

Words and Music by
Richard Rodgers & Oscar Hammerstein

MMO 2145

There's A Boat Dat's Leavin' Soon For N.Y.

from "Porgy & Bess"

Words and Music by
Ira Gershwin, George Gershwin,
Du bose Heyward, Dorothy Heyward

MMO 2145

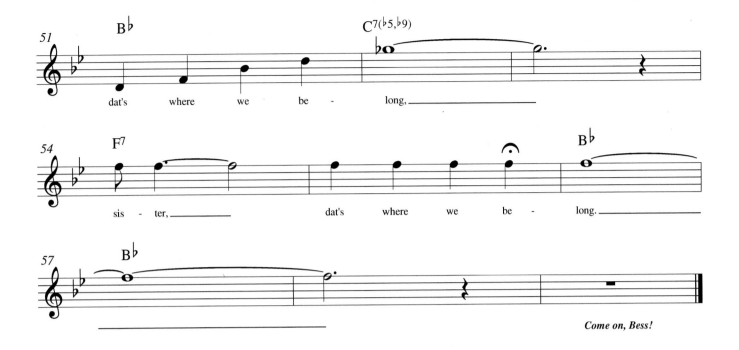

dat's where we be - long,

sis - ter, dat's where we be - long.

Come on, Bess!

Shipoopi

from "Music Man"

Words and Music by
Meredith Willson

way   to   sup - per.

Do,   re,   mi,   fa,   sol,   la,   si,   do,   si,

do.   Now   lit - tle   ol'   Sal   was a   No   Gal,   as

an - y - one   could   see.   Look - it   her   now.   She's a

Go - Gal,   who   on - ly   goes   for   me.   Squeeze

___   her   once   when   she   is - n't   look - in'.   If   you   get   a   squeeze   back   that's

fan - cy   cook - in'.   Once   more   for   a   pep - er - up - per.   She   will

nev - er   get   sore   on   her   way   to   sup - per.   Do,   re,   mi,   fa,

Bring Him Home
from "Les Miserables"

Words and Music by
Alain Boublil, Claude-Michel Schonberg &
Herbert Kretzmer

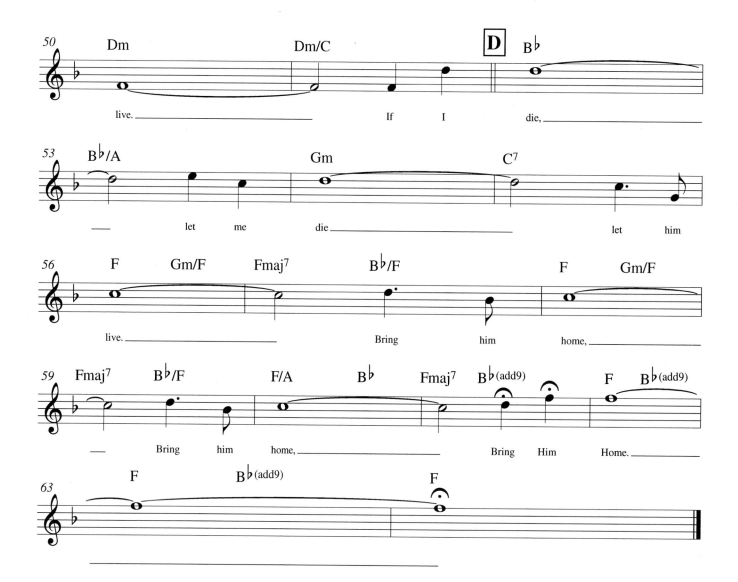

Music Minus One
50 Executive Boulevard • Elmsford, New York 10523-1325
914-592-1188 • e-mail: info@musicminusone.com
www.musicminusone.com

ISBN 978-1-941566-45-9